P9-EJK-740

BONSAI
and the
Japanese
garden

Applying the ancient Bonsai art
and Japanese Landscaping
to America's gardens

by
Kaneji Domoto
and George Kay

Countryside
Books

Kaneji Domoto — "Developing a Bonsai has been a very satisfying form of art to me. It has given me a great deal of pleasure creating beautiful shapes and giving character to ordinary plants. The Bonsai art is different from painting, sculpture or ceramics because it is a 'live art.' The Bonsai subject has seasonal growth which must be disciplined to a planned shape. It becomes a natural extension of my philosophy that any growing organism needs to be guided constantly in its growth to achieve character and beauty."

George R. Kay — "More than ever before the arts of Japanese landscaping and Bonsai are within the grasp of any seriously interested person. While adhering to the traditions that have fascinated the Japanese for centuries, our approach to these arts is nonetheless our own. This book facilitates the use of the Japanese past and adapts the art forms of the Japanese to a U.S. culture and thereby becomes a personal expression. As an active participant, you'll want to seek your own fresh expression within the disciplines set by tradition and nature."

LC Number 74-5161
ISBN: 0-87955-497-5
First Printing G

Table of Contents

PREFACE

Although there are many books and articles written about Bonsai and Japanese landscaping practices, most do not apply to the U.S. This is the primary reason for publishing this book

After 10 years of experimenting with and growing Bonsai, we've adapted the traditional Japanese techniques for determining soil type, seasonal care, repotting and trimming to American conditions.

Japanese Landscaping also requires many of the classical techniques and theories. Yet, again, we have made innovations that our culture and needs have imposed upon these ancient practices.

Innovations in both arts have been undertaken carefully and unobtrusively, as the following pages will illustrate.

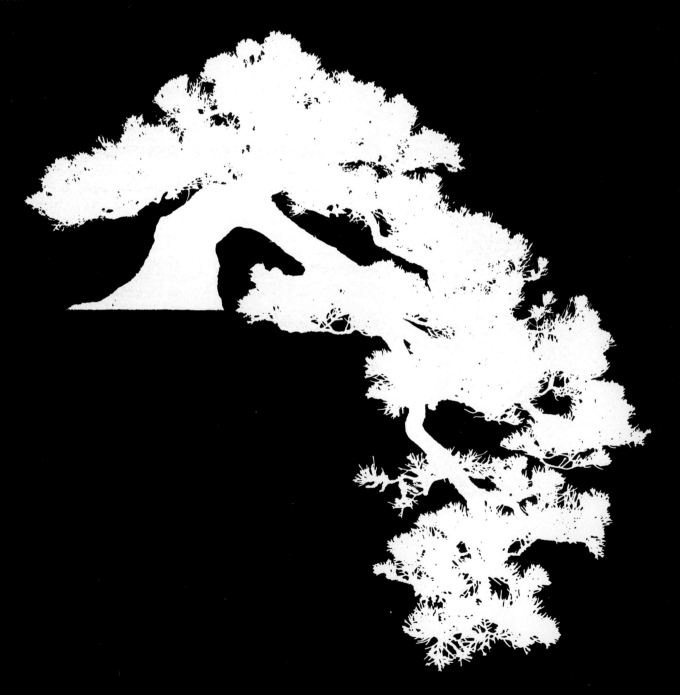

DEFINITION OF BONSAI

The Bonsai is a plant which has been shaped and dwarfed to the specifications of the gardener, then placed in a container carefully selected to complement the plant's form. Although natural dwarf plants can be used for Bonsai subjects, the main concern of this book are those dwarfed artificially or by the elements of nature.

BONSAI STYLES

Although there are many Bonsai styles, eight major classifications emerge:

1. **Single straight trunk [chokkan]**
2. **Single slanting trunk [shakkan]**
3. **Single cascading trunk [kengai]**
4. **Single gnarled trunk [moyogi]**
5. **Two or more trunks [kabudachi]**
6. **On a stone [ishitsuki]**
7. **Grouping or two or more subjects [yose-ue]**
8. **Interconnecting root systems [netsunari]**

BONSAI SIZE CLASSIFICATIONS

In addition to being identified by style, Bonsai are classified by size. Each of the eight styles can be seen in the following size classifications, where height is measured from the top of the container to the tip of growth.

1. **Mame Bonsai — Up to 3-in. in height.**
2. **Chu Bonsai — From 4-9 inches in height.**
3. **Dai Bonsai — From 10-15 inches in height.**
4. **Oh Bonsai — Taller than 16 inches.**

Selecting
a Bonsai subject

Pyracantha bonsai in fruit.

Selecting a good Bonsai subject is a lot like deciding which colt will make a great race horse. In both cases, hobbyists have identified certain traits or qualities that exist in all great specimens.

Great bonsai specimens have these attributes:

1. They possess great dramatic projection, personality and character. There is a balanced composition because of harmony and scale in relation to the container, roots, trunk, branches, leaves, fruit, flowers and rock outcroppings. The look of great age is desirable, yet the plant must project strength and good health.

2. Roots are exposed and appear gnarled from age. Lines formed by the roots complement those of the tree trunk.

3. Trunks are of large diameter, gnarled and scarred. Lichens and mosses at the tree's base add to the illusion of great age.

4. Branches complement the trunk's lines. Spacing allows the trunk to be revealed in a most advantageous way.

5. Leaves or needles are small and in proportion to the tree's size.
6. Fruits and flowers are scaled to the tree's size.

7. Drama is added through strategically-placed rock outcroppings. As in nature, the plant is placed beside, between or on top of the rock.

The intent of Bonsai training is creation of a beautiful tree. Although many plant species can be trained as Bonsai, the best results are achieved by careful selection of those having characteristics that lend themselves to the art.

Even with a knowledge of suitable plant materials, it often is difficult to select a formless plant and recognize its potential beauty. The best teacher is experience and a knowledge of what qualities good Bonsai subjects possess.

Bonsai beginners should start with containerized nursery-grown plants. Most of these plants, sold in one gallon cans or fibre pots, have well-developed root systems that allow severe root pruning. Pruning is necessary to fit these plants in the small Bonsai containers.

Nursery stock merchandised in this manner has the advantage of tolerating preliminary training at any time of the year. A careful inspection of plants with a group will reveal one or two specimens having trunks. The beginner should select one of these because of time saved in the training process.

An alternate method of selection is to collect a suitable subject from the wild. In areas of severe climatic change, plants are dwarfed by the elements. Among these millions of specimens there are a few that have the shape and quality to be a Bonsai.

Primary problem in this type of selection is transplanting. Because wilderness specimens are generally growing between rocks, it's nearly impossible to take enough of the root system for the transplanting to be a success.

Root pruning that takes several years and the right season also make this practice difficult.

Creation of a Bonsai

PRUNING YOUR BONSAI

With Bonsai, the pruning activity is a continuing one. From the time your subject has been selected and disciplining started it is never ending. Discipline begins with a severe pruning so that the trunk is exposed and branching limited to several limbs selected to express the desired form. Of prime importance in this early training is to avoid having branches growing from opposite sides of the trunk, or to have more than one branch at a node.* The initial pruning will make the tree look sparce, but it must be done or soon branches will grow together and you will be back at the beginning.

Pruning continues through the shaping or development period as well as into the maintenance period. When the plant has achieved the desired form, continued pruning is required to keep new growth disciplined.

Neglecting pruning just one season will ruin the plant's shape. A wild growing mass will replace the carefully scaled Bonsai.

Deciduous and evergreen plants must be pruned differently. Foliage can be stripped from the deciduous specimen and a new set of small leaves will appear. When five leaves emerge on a limb, cut it back until only two remain.

Deciduous plants can be cut back drastically so new shoots appear. Those that flower should be trimmed back after blooming has been completed. Branches should be cut close to the node so that the cut will heal cleanly.

Evergreens cannot be treated in this manner. Pines, for example, should be pruned at the time new needles start to unfold. New buds will form where pruning has taken place. Pruning during any other period requires complete removal of a branch. The stub left from any other cut between nodes will die.

Other evergreens, such as junipers and cedars, should be pruned con- stantly during the growing season. The constant pruning is required to keep branch length short as possible and terminals full.

WIRING OF BRANCHES AND TRUNK

To acquire the refined shape of a Bonsai, branches and sometimes the plant's trunk must be positioned. This is done by bending the branches into a shape that has been decided most aesthetic for that particular plant.

Copper wire is used to keep the branches and trunk in position. The wire should be thick enough to hold the branch yet pliable for ease of use.

The best way to wire the plant is to insert one end of the copper wire 1-2 inches into the soil near the trunk's base. Wind the wire in equal spirals 1-1/2 inches apart. Although the wire should firmly hold the plant in position, do not allow it to cut into the bark. Continue this procedure until all branches have been wired.

Wire should be left on the plant for a year. After this period branches are permanently in position.

An alternate method for achieving desired shape is to bend a metal rod into the shape desired for trunk or branch. The plant is shaped to the metal rod by winding string around the trunk or branch and rod.

Both methods are means to an end, such as splints used to set broken bones. Technique pales in importance to ultimate shape.

SELECTING THE CORRECT CONTAINER

Bonsai containers are glazed and hard-grained to eliminate filtering of water through the pot. Drainage is provided by a hole or holes in the bottom of the container. Color should be subdued and preferably earthen.

The container must be selected carefully for size and shape in addition to texture and color. Size must be scaled so that the illusion of a large tree is maintained. Its shape should complement the tree's form.

Bonsai containers can be purchased in rectangular, square, hexagonal, round and elliptical shapes. They vary in size from two inches in diameter for miniature plants up to 24 inches for the very large ones. Although many containers are no more than an inch deep, the average depth is nearly 4 inches.

The container you choose is determined by the Bonsai subject selected. Shape, foliage color and fruit size are important factors. Choosing the right container creates harmony in every aspect of the overall composition.

Do not select a container that is too large for the subject. Remember, the Bonsai is to receive most attention. A distracting container because of shape, color or size, will destroy the harmony that is necessary for good Bonsai composition.

POINTS TO REMEMBER

1. Size and shape of subject.
2. Needle or leaf, color of subject and size of leaf.
3. Color of container.
4. Shape and size of container.
5. Drainage.
6. Quality of container.

SOIL REQUIREMENTS

The best Bonsai soil mix consists of fertile garden soil, sharp sand and peat moss. Various percentages of these components will provide good results. Yet, it's a good idea to experiment until a rich, porous soil is achieved.

Soil media such as clay, compost, aged manure or bog moss may produce satisfactory results with certain plant types, but in most cases a mix of the garden loam, sand and peat moss will prove ideal.

* Node — an enlarged portion of the stem from which leaves and branches emerge.

FERTILIZATION

The small container restricts the amount of food available for a growing, healthy plant. To keep your Bonsai at peak appearance, it is essential to apply small amounts of fertilizer frequently.

A plant left unfertilized will begin to look anemic, and require a great deal of care until normal color, vigor and general atmosphere of health reappear.

Most fertilizers are applied during the active growing season spanning spring and summer months. Organic fertilizers produce best results, especially those that release nutrients slowly.

Another method of feeding the Bonsai is the application of diluted liquid fertilizer every other week.

Fertilizing during winter months or during dormancy is not only unnecessary, but wasteful since the plants are not needing fertilizer at these times.

BONSAI PLACEMENT

When you are ready to place the plant in the container, great care must be taken to locate the one spot dictated by good composition.

Most specimens are asymmetrical in form; therefore, rarely will the plant be placed in the center of the container.

Although there are rules to help with composition, none will seem to apply when you have the subject in hand. Timidity in design is the customary fault of the beginner. Therefore, overemphasize your design concept.

This is necessary at the start because the growing plant tends to destroy the sharp definition and grow into a formless green glob.

After you have pruned your Bonsai, selected the correct container, planted the Bonsai in the proper soil, placed the plant in the container, wired the branches and trunk, you are ready for the finishing touches such as rock outcropping, moss and lichens. These elements should be used to supplement the design. Furthermore, the moss and the lichens are used for the practical

Select a small containerized specimen plant, in this case a spreading form of juniper.

Tip the plant upside down to remove it from the container.

Use a pointed stick to free soil around the roots.

purpose of keeping the soil from eroding as well as acting as moisture indicators. If the moss is dry, the Bonsai is lacking water.

Stones selected must be scaled to complement overall composition of container and plant. I prefer to exaggerate the scale of the stone in relation to the container and plant. They should not distract by being ornate. A search of shaded damp areas will yield moss and lichens suitable for

their role as ground cover.

No matter how clear written instructions can be, the actual reality of making a Bonsai leaves great doubts in many areas. Usually it becomes a decision of cutting a branch or leaving it alone. Ponder this. Do not feel the need to rush to a decision. A month may pass — perhaps several months. One day you will know what to do. With this sort of decision making, one becomes appreciative of fine Bonsai.

Cut back the roots to approximately one-half inch from container wall.

Begin to branch prune.

Now spaces are being seen in addition to the appearance of the tree's trunk. Additional trimming refines the plant's new shape.

Following the pruning process, a correct container must be found. A trial planting is made in a tall container. But because the plant is horizontal in shape, a low horizontal container is selected.

As with houseplants, Bonsai containers require drainage holes. A screen placed in the bottom of the container holds soil in place.

Because the plant has an asymmetrical form, plant your Bonsai carefully, and off-center. Carefully place soil around the plant's roots. Firm the soil to eliminate air pockets.

Mound soil from the container's edge up to the plant. This small hill is a desirable feature in making a Bonsai.

*Consider the total composition, trim additionally if required, then begin
wiring branches into desired positions and shapes.*

When starting to wire, place one and a half inches of wire into the soil,
then begin wrapping the wire around the trunk in even coils. Although
the wire should hold the trunk firmly, it should not be tight.

Continue the wire coils around the first secondary branch, careful not to damage leaflets or small branches. Follow the branch to the end and cut the wire.

Bend the wired branch to the desired position.

Start a second wire next to the first. Following the same spiral up the trunk, branch off at another secondary limb.

Wire this branch to the end, cut the wire and bend to desired position and shape.

Continue the process until all secondary branches have been wired and bent into the desired shape.

Step back to inspect the entire composition. Invariably, you'll want to rearrange branches to achieve the best appearance.

Place a stone in the container to complement the composition. The stone must be shaped to enhance the lines of the branches and trunk of the plant. It also must look attractive from all viewing angles. To achieve the look of a natural outcropping, the stone must be partially buried.

The Bonsai is now complete with the exception of moss placement on exposed soil surfaces and some minor trimming.

WATERING REQUIREMENTS

Your Bonsai water requirement is determined day to day by weather conditions which include temperature, humidity, wind and sun. During hot days the water requirements may change from hour to hour.

Factors playing a role in watering frequency include: (1) The amount of soil in container; (2) Size and type of plant; (3) Time of year; (4) Location; and (5) Climatic conditions, including temperature, humidity, wind and sun.

Season and climatic conditions have great impact on watering activities. On hot summer days more than one watering may be necessary, while during cool rainy periods, watering may be unnecessary for days at a time.

Where Bonsai are wintered in complete dormancy in a cold frame, window well, etc., the winter may pass without the need to water. In areas receiving excessive rainfall, a shelter may be required for protection.

Watering can be accomplished in several ways:
(1) Watering the soil directly.
(2) Watering the foliage with adequate water falling to the soil.
(3) Placement of the Bonsai in a tray of water and allowing it to stand for a period of time.
(4) Spray mist watering.

Each watering should be effective enough so the entire soil mass is moist. Overwatering at one time should not be of concern. Proper soil mixture will allow excess moisture to drain away.

The best method for watering newly-planted or transplanted Bonsai is foliage spray misting.

INSECT AND DISEASE PROBLEMS

Bonsai plants are subjected to identical insect and disease problems as plants in your garden. Because the plant is scaled down, the problem is unlikely to be as great.

Simple action often can be taken to protect the Bonsai from insect infestation. Often a strong water spray can be used to wash insects from the plant. When only a few insects are apparent, removal by hand is best and easiest.

Where a major problem does occur, however, a commercial insecticide should be used. Pamphlets describing these pests and best control are available at most garden centers.

Plant diseases are more difficult to control. Because most of these diseases are harbored in the soil, a packaged product should be obtained from a reputable nursery. Such soils have been steam cured to prevent disease spread.

When the Bonsai is inspected frequently, the chance of any major infestation is small.

WINTERING OF BONSAI

The northern Bonsai enthusiast may need a cold frame during winter months. Containers should be buried in humus or compost so the soil does not dry out.

On warm sunny days the glass frame should be raised to prevent heat buildup. Morning waterings may be necessary during these warm winter periods.

Bonsai in shaded shelters or cold frames do not require frequent waterings during the winter. The primary purposes of these shelters are to eliminate harmful variations in temperature and to protect against winter winds.

When the Bonasi collection is small, window wells will provide the same kind of protection. Below the Mason-Dixon line, temperatures are mild enough so that these precautions are not necessary.

REPOTTING AND ROOT PRUNING BONSAI

Every two years the Bonsai is carefully taken out of the container and the roots are pruned back to leave 1/2 inch of space between the root mass and the container. (in warm climates like Florida and California, root pruning on some plants is a yearly process).

Roots are pruned to prevent the Bonsai from becoming pot bound. The new soil added encourages new root growth which benefits the foliage growth.

When cutting the roots, use a sharp scissors so that cuts are clean. Clean cuts heal faster and encourage growth of new fine hair roots. The plant depends on these small roots for food and water.

Space between the roots and container is filled with new soil. Repotting can be done with the same soil mix of peat moss, sand and loam as was used when the plant began training. This combination has adequate humus to retain moisture and enough porosity to drain the excess. Because the new soil is fertile, supplemental feeding is not necessary for several months.

To prevent air pockets from occurring when potting, a pointed stick is used to poke soil between and under the roots.

The best time to repot is spring, although evergreens respond to it both spring and fall.

Repotting is not an annual task. Rarely is it needed more than every 2-5 years. The only way to determine the proper time for repotting is to take the Bonsai out of its container and inspect the root system. After two years of root growth the root system usually is closely intertwined and there is little danger of the soil falling away.

Step by step, here is the best repotting method.

1. Carefully remove the Bonsai from its container.
2. Remove soil from the roots with a pointed stick.
3. Cut roots back to a point that would be 1/2 inch from the container's sides.
4. After cleaning the container, place a wire screen over the drainage holes and add a layer of gravel on the bottom.
5. Water the Bonsai by soaking the soil mass in a tub of water until it becomes saturated.
6. Position the plant and tamp new potting soil around and under the roots with a pointed stick.
7. Place the repotted Bonsai in a lightly shaded area, protected from drying winds. Mist sprays applied several times a day for the first week also will guard against the plant's tendency to dry out. Gradually expose the Bonsai to more sunshine over a 2-3 week period.

DISPLAYING THE BONSAI

Setting aside a definite area for the care of Bonsai during the warm months will facilitate their growth. Such a shelter should be designed with expansion in mind.

Wood is the best material for constructing overhead lath and tables. There should be screens on the sides for wind protection. Bamboo or live evergreens provide a good backdrop. Whatever material is used, the background should be neutral so Bonsai are showed off to best advantage.

Combined with a work area, the shelter can become the nerve center for your entire garden.

Shelters provide:
1. Ease in the care of Bonsai by having tables and shelves at the correct height for viewing and working.
2. Screening from the sun.
3. Wind control.
4. A possible area for overwintering.
5. A showcase for specimen display.

OUTDOOR vs. INDOOR CARE

The question often is asked, "May I grow Bonsai inside?" Although the answer is "Yes," success will be limited and frustrations manifold. If indoor culture is necessary realize that results will not be the same as when the plant is grown outdoors under ideal conditions. Traditionally Bonsai plants are outdoor plants.

Indoor Bonsai seldom attain the beauty achieved with outdoor care. It remains too difficult for outdoor conditions to be simulated. An aesthetically beautiful Bonsai will be one developed outdoors.

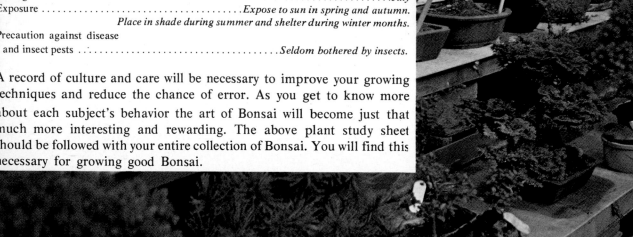

SAMPLE

BONSAI CULTURE AND CARE STUDY SHEET

Plant name . . . . *Japanese Maple*
Soil requirement . . . . *Mostly loam*
Frequency of transplanting . . . . *Once every three years*
Transplanting season . . . . *Before buds unfold in spring*
Precautions necessary during transplanting . . . . *Remove all old soil*
Watering requirement . . . . *Likes a fair amount of water*
Fertilizer requirement . . . . *Once a month*
Pruning and control of new growth . . . . *Cut back majority of new growth*
Trimming of branches . . . . *Before new growth in spring*
Wiring . . . . *July*
Exposure . . . . *Expose to sun in spring and autumn.*
Place in shade during summer and shelter during winter months.
Precaution against disease
and insect pests . . . . *Seldom bothered by insects.*

A record of culture and care will be necessary to improve your growing techniques and reduce the chance of error. As you get to know more about each subject's behavior the art of Bonsai will become just that much more interesting and rewarding. The above plant study sheet should be followed with your entire collection of Bonsai. You will find this necessary for growing good Bonsai.

This large collection of Bonsai is wintered in a cool greenhouse. Northern climates require substantial winter protection. During the warm months, they can be removed from this greenhouse and displayed on raised wood tables.

The above display of Bonsai is at a production Bonsai nursery. The beginner should visit one to learn technique and variety of form.

Suitable plants for Bonsai

BROADLEAF EVERGREENS

Azalea	*Azalea*	Attractive flowers and leaves
Buxus microphylla	*Boxwood*	Attractive waxy leaves
Camellia japonica	*Camellia*	Attractive flowers and leaves
Illex crenata	*Japanese Holly*	Excellent leaves and blue black berries.
Nandina domestica	*Nandina*	Attractive red berries. Young foliage tinged with red.
Pyracantha coccinea	*Firethorn*	Attractive red or orange berries.
Quercus ilex	*Holly Oak*	Interesting leaves and bark.

Azalea

DECIDUOUS SHRUBS

Aronia arbutifolia	*Red Chokeberry*	Red berries and attractive fall foliage color.
Azalea	*Azalea*	Attractive flowers and leaves.
Berberis	*Barberry*	Berries and attractive fall foliage color.
Caragana arborescens	*Siberian Pea Shrub*	Attractive foliage.
Chaenomeles japonica	*Flowering Quince*	Attractive flowers.
Cotoneaster	*Cotoneaster*	Attractive flowers, berries and fall foliage color.
Ligustrum vulgare	*Common Privet*	Small leaves
Punica granatum nana	*Dwarf Pomegranate*	Attractive orange fruit.
Spiraea thunbergi	*Thunberg Spirea*	White flowers and good texture.

Cotoneaster

DECIDUOUS VINES

Parthenocissus tricuspidata	*Vietch's Boston Ivy*	Attractive fall foliage color.
Wisteria sinensis	*Wisteria*	Attractive flowers and leaves.

Boston Ivy

Red Barberry

NEEDLED EVERGREENS

Cedrus atlantica	*Atlas Cedar*	Foliage interest
Chamaecyparis	*Cypress*	Foliage interest
Cryptomeria japonica	*Cryptomeria*	Needle interest and form.
Juniperus chinensis San Jose	*San Jose Juniper*	Variation in needles.
Juniperus chinensis Sargent	*Sargent Juniper*	Texture of foliage.
Juniperus procumbens nana	*Dwarf Japanese Juniper*	Total appearance.
Juniperus virginiana	*Eastern Red Cedar* [Juniper Varieties]	Foliage color. Deep greens to blue.
Picea glauca conica	*Dwarf Alberta Spruce*	Foliage interest
Picea jezoensis	*Yeddo Spruce*	Gray bark and interesting buds.
Picea abies nidiformis	*Birds Nest Spruce*	Small needles and natural dwarf appearance.
Pinus cembra	*Swiss Stone Pine*	Interesting bark and attractive needles.
Pinus flexilis	*Limber Pine*	Fissured bark in old age.
Pinus nigra	*Austrian Pine*	Gray bark and dark green needles.
Pinus parviflora	*Japanese White Pine*	Fissured bark and bluish green needles.
Pinus pumila	*Japanese Stone Pine*	Entire composition is interesting.
Pinus sylvestris	*Scotch Pine*	Bark and needle arrangement.
Pinus thunbergi	*Japanese Black Pine*	Blackish gray bark.

DECIDUOUS TREES

Acer buergerianum	*Trident Maple*	Bark and foliage color in fall.
Acer campestre	*Hedge Maple*	Interesting bark and fall foliage color.
Acer ginnala	*Amur Maple*	Interesting bark and fall foliage color.
Acer palmatum	*Japanese Maple*	Entire composition is attractive.
Amelanchier canadensis	*Serviceberry*	Entire composition is attractive.
Betula	*Birch*	Bark
Carpinus caroliniana	*American Hornbeam*	Bark and fall foliage color.
Celtis occidentalis	*Hackberry*	Bark
Cercidiphyllum japonicum	*Katsura Tree*	Fall foliage color.
Crataegus	*Hawthorns*	Berries
Ginkgo biloba	*Ginkgo*	Leaves, buds and bark.
Fagus sylvatica	*Beech*	Buds and bark.
Larix decidua	*European Larch*	Leaves
Larix leptolepos	*Japanese Larch*	Leaves
Liquidambar styraciflua	*Sweet Gum*	Leaves
Malus	*Flowering Crabs*	Flowers and fruit
Prunus mume	*Japanese Apricot*	Flowers
Prunus subhirtella	*Flowering Cherry*	Flowers and bark
Salix alba tristis	*Weeping Willow*	Bark and leaves
Zelkova serrata	*Gray Bark Elm*	Bark

Scotch Pine

Katsura Tree

Ginkgo

Japanese Maple

Far Left: This Blaauw Juniper bonsai demonstrates numerous trunks growing from a single crown. Note the branch that is dead. The Japanese call this Jin and it is highly desirable because it adds the look of great age to the plant. This specimen is 20 inches tall and 10 years old. Top Left: Although the trunks are rather thin, this is the beginning of an extremely good Chinese Juniper bonsai. The plant is approximately 15 years of age. Center Left: This San Jose Juniper is a low growing type with natural interesting branching. Windswept and cascade bonsai styles are easy to do with this juniper. The subject shown is only 7 years old and displays the potential of being a great Bonsai subject with age. Bottom left: The art of Saikei (Living landscapes) is best illustrated in this photo. This art differs from Bonsai because it allows greater freedom in the use of plants, stone, moss and statuary. Because of this freedom, many unusual and outstanding landscapes are created. Chinese junipers are planted in the illustrated Saikei composition. Upper Right: The popular Pfitzer Juniper illustrates the windswept appearance of a tree growing along the U. S. Pacific Coast. This specimen is 7 years old. Above: The windswept, cascading appearance of this Bonsai is reminiscent of craggy bluffs and beach landscapes. Some Junipers lend themselves to this style.

32

Upper left, page 32: Cypress is used extremely well in this composition. The use of several plants, gravel and elevation changes represent extensions of the bonsai art. Lower left, page 32: The Hinoki Cypress makes a good bonsai subject because of its dwarf habit and luxurious foliage. This particular bonsai is 11 years old and 9 inches tall. Lower right, page 32: An interesting effect is created by this Atlas Cedar which is 12 years old and 12 inches tall. Upper left, page 33: Rugged beauty is demonstrated by this Alberta Spruce bonsai. Lower left, page 33: The versatility of the Alberta Spruce is exhibited by this multiple plant composition, giving the illusion of a miniature forest. The plants are 8 years old and 8 inches tall. Right, page 33: The use of elevation and plant height variations creates a third dimensional effect in this miniature spruce forest.

Above: This cotoneaster is a former grand prize winner at the Midwest Bonsai show. Twenty years of age, the specimen has been trained as a bonsai for 14 years.

Above Right: An azalea which has been trained as an attractive cascade style bonsai provides interesting leaf texture and colorful flowers.

Below Right: Finding the correct rock was as important as finding an attractive plant for this composition. Boxwood, a broadleaf evergreen, was a well chosen selection for this bonsai.

Above: An exceptional Red Barberry bonsai. Although trained for just a few years, it is extremely handsome. Upper Right: The Hackberry is normally a street tree growing to 75 ft. or more. The illustrated specimen is approximately 35 years old and only 13 inches tall. Extreme Right and Below: Two Zelkova specimens. The one above is two-trunked and made as part of a mountainous composition. The manner in which the tree was placed on a rock demonstrates the owner's great skill. Below is a venerable specimen 18 inches tall and 28 years old. Foliage and trunk interest is superb. The alternate shades of green add to the plant's interest.

Much of the Hackberry's recent popularity for Bonsai culture can be traced to an Army captain's search for suitable Bonsai subjects in the Tennessee countryside during 1958. He noticed cattle grazing near mature Hackberry trees. Below the mature trees, volunteer seedlings were repeatedly being topped. Many of the volunteers were 12-15 inches tall, had trunk diameters to 2 inches and estimated to be 25 years of age. With permission, several of the trees were successfully moved and transplanted. They are now displayed in several private collections.

37

Left and Below: The Japanese call the Trident Maple To-Kaede. It provides beauty throughout the growing season with lush green leaves turning into a variety of scarlet hues with the onset of fall. This bonsai's age is 30 and stature is 17 inches. Right: The Japanese maple is prized for its many trunks. This old Momiji is 20 inches tall and 35 years old.

Gardens with a Japanese influence

Americans have always utilized trees, shrubs, rock and water to form their gardens, but these elements' use has been in the context of European and British experience.

These same elements are basic to Japanese gardens, yet their composition is extremely different. What we have attempted to do is combine much of our gardening tradition with Japanese ideas, resulting in refreshing garden design concepts.

Just as the Japanese imported ideas from China and incorporated them into their culture, we have studied Japanese gardens and have incorporated their elements into our culture.

To illustrate, most Japanese gardens are a composition of green upon green. Trees and shrubs; both deciduous and evergreen have blooms but they are incidental in the garden design in that these blooms last perhaps for two weeks. Sometimes these plants are prized because of the brief period of bloom. Annuals and perennials, mainstays of American Gardens, are not usually found in Japanese gardens. Yet, we have been extremely successful in introducing into an oriental design dwarf marigolds, zinnias, petunias, verbenas, creeping phlox, alyssums, asters, candytuft, dwarf irises and primroses.

Garden Design

Of the many elements that go into making a successful Japanese Garden, the most important is stone. The permanent quality of stone is well known. Altho stones do not grow like plants, they also do not deteriorate and die like plants. Plants have been vandalized the night after they had been planted; but never has a stone been vandalized or graffittized. Once stones are placed in harmonious composition, they remain in that carefully placed composition. The stones do not grow out of shape. The stones do not need any maintenance.

In large gardens, the stones should be large to be in scale. In small areas, the stones should be proportionately small to be in harmony. This does not mean that in small spaces one should use only small stones. In fact, some outstanding small gardens use huge stones as accent.

Proportions used in Japanese flower arranging also are employed for rock compositions. This is the arrangement of tall, medium and short stones in the heaven, earth and man combination.

Ground preparation is extremely important in rock garden design. The earth must be shaped into hills, flat land, pond or lake areas. Fiberglass liners or concrete must be utilized for water retention.

A waterfall should originate from the high ground. The stone grouping at the waterfall is most important. Avoid the monotony of equal size stones. Many sizes and shapes add interest to the composition and suggest how the waterfall would appear in nature.

Although stone groupings have strong sculptural appeal the addition of plants complement these compositions. Their introduction should follow the time-consuming rock work.

Plantlife must be selected carefully as to size, shape, texture, color, flowers and fruit. Selecting the correct plants for given areas will reduce the amount of maintenance required.

When a low, creeping evergreen is desired, use one of the many junipers. They are excellent when a sunny area in the garden is present and depending upon variety, needle tone ranges from a silvery green to blue.

Rhododendrons and azaleas are ideal when broadleaf flowering evergreens are required in shaded areas of the garden. The rough texture of many tall evergreens such as cryptomeria, scotch pine, or Japanese Black Pine may be desirable. On the other hand, smooth textured trees may provide the proper accent. Examples of these are hemlock, yew, white pine, cedar and cypress.

Whatever the planting arrangement and overall garden composition, an object in the foreground will increase sense of depth. This technique is used extensively in photography where a branch or tree trunk frames a distant view. Such is true in landscape design. A feeling of depth must be created either with a foreground tree or grouping.

Backgrounds also must be planned with care. Not only does a good background planting contain the scene created, but it also shuts out objectional views. An imaginative planting can be achieved if its depth is varied and the line curved. Never place your background straight along the property line.

Even with careful plant selection, special accent trees and shrubs must be shaped and pruned to maintain scale. Because growth is rapid and luxuriant, plants will become unmanageable if a regular pruning program is not followed.

These are general suggestions for garden making. On the following pages are garden ideas that can be adapted for use in your plan.

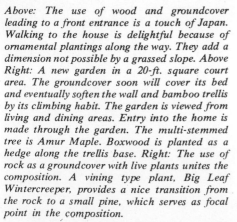

Above: The use of wood and groundcover leading to a front entrance is a touch of Japan. Walking to the house is delightful because of ornamental plantings along the way. They add a dimension not possible by a grassed slope. Above Right: A new garden in a 20-ft. square court area. The groundcover soon will cover its bed and eventually soften the wall and bamboo trellis by its climbing habit. The garden is viewed from living and dining areas. Entry into the home is made through the garden. The multi-stemmed tree is Amur Maple. Boxwood is planted as a hedge along the trellis base. Right: The use of rock as a groundcover with live plants unites the composition. A vining type plant, Big Leaf Wintercreeper, provides a nice transition from the rock to a small pine, which serves as focal point in the composition.

Far Left: The weeping Japanese Cherry has form that is perfect for introducing tranquility into the garden. Left: A low Japanese Yew hedge directs the eye to a carved stone water basin. The container is subdued in color and does not glare. Shape and coloring were important factors so the basin would complement the slate walkway. Above: The use of wood as a fence and patio, along with earth-colored gravel, is attractive yet restful. Adding tranquility are lantern, wood-bench, rock outcroppings and plantings.

Constructing a pool garden

Stone sculptured gardens are different from other landscape compositions because plans cannot be followed in detail. Ultimate design is greatly dependent upon the shapes of stones gathered for the job.

From the moment the first stone is placed, basic design has been determined. Yet, the quality of stone sculptured gardens depends on the person placing the stones. Because it is a very personal art, this placement cannot be delegated.

A large sculptured garden recently was constructed for Japan Airlines in New York City. Although a commercial project, its construction is classic. A step-by-step explanation follows:

The first step in making a stone sculptured pool garden is to outline the shape with stakes. The outline must be large enough so stones can be placed on the perimeter. Earth is excavated so that the deepest area will be approximately 2-1/2 feet.

Concrete is poured to form the shell. Stones are placed inside the shell, insuring the retention of water.

Welded wire fabric reinforces the cement of a permanent pool. The pool's final shape is much different from the shell because of rock placement along the perimeter. In many instances, rocks can be placed when the cement is wet.

But the usual procedure is to place them after the concrete has set. Stones are propped into position by placing smaller ones beneath. Any void remaining under the stone is filled with concrete.

The second stone is placed to complement the accent stone. Remaining stones follow, complementing the composition.

Placement begins with the largest stone, because the eye is automatically drawn to it. This stone is placed with great care because it sets the mood for the remaining stone placements and resulting composition.

A large tree in the left foreground gives depth to the garden. Various lanterns and pagoda are accent points and are carefully located to weld the garden composition together.

Decide what face is most attractive and place the stone so this side can be seen from the main viewing angle. In other words, if the main view of the waterfall is from a study window, the desired face should be visible.

The completed garden.

As a person walks through the garden, the accent points compose differently, but are aesthetically pleasing ... ever changing and yet forever delightful. Because of the temporary nature of the garden, wood chips were used instead of soil.

Even when one of the major accent points is close by, the garden's composition holds together aesthetically.

A close-up of the waterfall reveals motion and the sparkle of sunlight. The one thing it cannot show is sound. This music is serene, yet different in every garden.

A Stone Sculptured Garden

This garden is designed in the style of the famous Ryoanji garden in Japan. There is no slavish reproduction of the original temple garden. Because stones are different, the composition has a completely different character. Yet the result is serene.

Largest of the stones was placed first. Its face was directed to the main view. The second group of stones was subordinately composed to the first group. Although the second group is complete within itself it relates closely to the first group.

Garden Ideas

DOORWAY GARDEN

As a guest approaches this house the immediate garden composition defines the main entrance. A Japanese table pine creates interest and delight for the viewer. Japanese spurge (pachysandra) is used beneath the pine, bordered front and rear by cobblestone 5-7 inches in diameter laid on 3 inches of fine sand.

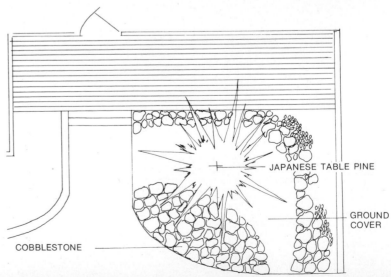

JAPANESE TABLE PINE

GROUND COVER

COBBLESTONE

GARDEN PATH

A garden path is more aesthetic circuitous than straight. Not only does it allow a better view of garden highlights, but it is more natural. This design shows the effect of a simple composition. Wood planks, large and small stones, ivy, wild ginger, rhododendron and a lantern are design elements.

LANTERN ACCENT

When the edging line becomes long, an accent should be introduced to break monotony. This lantern adds an interesting break and a natural one. Because poorly-placed accents create a contrived look, experiment. Plantlife used in this composition are dwarf Japanese juniper, bronxensis forsythia and bigleaf wintercreeper.

ISLAND GARDEN

A positive border of palings with stones as terminals form one side of this island garden. Planned in conjunction with an existing tree, the garden utilizes juniper, mugho pine and Japanese spurge as groundcovers. A pleasing variety of textures emerge.

SIMPLE ELEMENTS

An interesting composition of three elements. Statue, stone and mugho pine are in good balance. Because of the pine's growth, the balance may eventually be altered or destroyed. A yellowwood tree in bloom provides a canopy.

MULTIPLE STEM PINE

An accent can be a single specimen plant such as this Japanese table pine. Because there is plenty of room for growth, its value will increase with each passing year. Cobblestone used at the base provides additional interest and attraction to the planting. Carrying out the natural stone theme is the sidewalk having a pebble surface. One can view this pine from both upper and lower areas of the house. The pine's multiple stems add depth to the composition.

Left: This Japanese bridge is old, yet still functional. It was built more than 70 years ago, yet is strong. A less elaborate one is shown elsewhere in this book and may be best to span your pond. In addition to obvious function a bridge can be a place to get a new perspective on the garden. Below: Attractive older gardens are the result of careful plant selection and pruning so scale is maintained. In the foreground is a carefully pruned Green Japanese Maple.

ROCK PLACEMENTS

A simple stone composition provides the focal point in this raised planter. Pyramidal arborvitae frame the planter on three sides. Chinaberry vine is allowed to spill over the 3 x 14 inch wood planking. Thyme is used around the partially buried rocks and gravel covers the remaining soil surface.

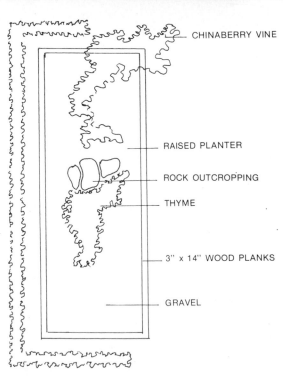

CHINABERRY VINE

RAISED PLANTER

ROCK OUTCROPPING

THYME

3" x 14" WOOD PLANKS

GRAVEL

COURT GARDEN

Passing through a gate creates a pleasing surprise of varied scenery. The wealth of plants and garden features produce the effect of many gardens within one.

Part of the court's gracefulness is created by the wooden bench and narrowness of the path leading to the sitting area. The existing multiple stem plant is common witchhazel which adds stability to the area. Its thread-like flowers bloom in late October and often during much of November. Their color is yellow and a delight to see at that time of year.

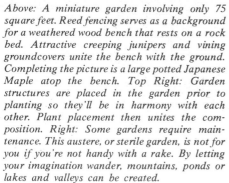

Above: A miniature garden involving only 75 square feet. Reed fencing serves as a background for a weathered wood bench that rests on a rock bed. Attractive creeping junipers and vining groundcovers unite the bench with the ground. Completing the picture is a large potted Japanese Maple atop the bench. Top Right: Garden structures are placed in the garden prior to planting so they'll be in harmony with each other. Plant placement then unites the composition. Right: Some gardens require maintenance. This austere, or sterile garden, is not for you if you're not handy with a rake. By letting your imagination wander, mountains, ponds or lakes and valleys can be created.

VIEWING GARDEN

The flagstone wall is softened with a weeping red jade crabapple. Softening also is achieved with sedum between the wall and wood beam bench.

Climbing the wall directly in back of the bench is bigleaf wintercreeper. It also serves as a means for reducing boldness.

This section of the same garden was treated to reduce the monotony of existing flagstone. Wood palings were used to retain the slope, descending from a wooded area. Cutleaf sumac is the fineleaved plant in the background.

A SIMPLE BRIDGE

It's a delight to walk over a simple bridge crossing a small waterway. A bit of planting adds a softening charm to the composition.

The grass-like plant in the water is cat-tail. Bigleaf wintercreeper is used as groundcover. Wood palings 5-7 inches in diameter are trenched in place up to half their length. Pebbles are used on the pond's bottom. Materials used to construct the bridge are 3 x 12 inch rough sawn planks supported by 4 x 4 inch wood posts and 2 x 4 inch cross members.

Using design elements correctly

Successful gardens emerge because the designer has known how to handle structures and plantlife. Here are some suggestions for their use and placement.

Fences

Fences provide privacy, security, weather control, planting backgrounds, create interest and identify property borders. Styles and materials abound. Selection must depend on the fence's purpose and placement in the garden.

Benches

Benches provide not only a place to rest, but are a decorative part of the garden as well. Their proper placement creates a restful appearance in addition to a functional role. When used with other garden structures, an otherwise dull area can be made attractive.

Retaining Slopes

Whenever there is a change in elevation, an opportunity arises to create interest not possible on a flat area. Retaining structures of flagstone, rocks, wood palings, brick, concrete block and wood beams provide areas for plantings of trees, shrubs, evergreens or even mass plantings of annuals and perennials.

Walks and Steps

The smooth, finished appearance of concrete often clashes with good garden design. If concrete must be used, score or broom the surface. Another idea is to expose aggregate on the surface. Alternate materials for walkways include flagstone, paving brick, slate and solid wood beams. Where there is little traffic, bark chips, wood rounds, flat-surfaced rocks and gravel work well.

Patios

The outdoor room or patio can be a garden asset if well-planned. A slab of concrete, with its stark appearance and propensity for cracking, is not the answer. To eliminate the possibility of cracking, use some kind of dividing material to create small sections. Redwood or cedar beams work well for this purpose. Concrete can be colored, its surface roughed or aggregate exposed. Wood, flagstone, paving brick or rock also work well in patio compositions.

Statuary

When positioned correctly, statuary has a place in the garden. Interesting settings can be created when statuary is used in conjunction with plantlife such as a small tree or groundcover. Its charm will be greater, however, if not in full view.

Garden Lighting

Lighting makes outdoor areas safer, more useful and attractive. Another dimension is added to garden beauty and the home's interior seems more spacious. Structures, such as statuary, fences, gates, pools, walks, steps and attractive walls can be lighted. Plantlife is especially attractive backlighted. Fixtures should be concealed and yield a soft light for best results.

Pools

Water creates tranquility within the garden, but only when its flow is soft. The manner in which the waterfall or pool is constructed will determine how successful the builder has been in attaining this goal. A blatant splashing noise is not pleasant or tranquil.

Shadow Patterns

Trees and shrubs with interesting branching habits can create unusual and beautiful designs on neighboring fences and walls. These shadow patterns should be considered in the plant's placement and resulting overall composition.

Unusual Trees

Multiple stemmed small trees, irregular growing pines or groupings of larger-than-average shrubs lend themselves to corners of buildings and spacious walls.

Texture

When planting the garden, place shrubs and trees so there is a graduation in leaf textures and color. This, of course, does not hold true where an accent plant is desired.

Groupings

Foundation plantings in multiples of three or more are desirable. Multiple plantings also are appropriate in background and boundary plantings. Groundcover plants must be used in mass for best effect.

Potted Patio Plants

A container of chrysanthemums, petunias or geraniums can be an attractive addition to patio decor. A more permanent approach is the planting of pine or juniper. The use of interesting deciduous small-growing plants such as cutleaf sumac or red jade crabapple would be delightful.

Plant Characteristics

Plants that have more than one interesting feature should be selected for the garden because each season highlights a different plant part. For example, Washington Hawthorn flowers during early spring. Lush green foliage replaces flowers during the summer. Berries appear in late summer followed by the changing of foliage color to a golden-orange. The tree is interesting in winter months as well because of attractive branching habit. Flowers, berries, foliage changes, bark, branching habit and leaf texture combine to increase the plant's seasonality.

Unfortunately few of us have a great deal of land to work with, as demonstrated above by Cherry trees along a quiet lagoon. Much can be done in a small area. At far left is a Japanese water well, which can be fashioned with stone and wood strips. Left, is a rock outcropping effectively planted with hardy sedums. A water pool is shown at right, constructed with bamboo and hollowed rock. Fern and lantern complete the scene.

Plants to create the Oriental feeling

DECIDUOUS LARGE TREES

FOR
Accent

Entrances

Spacious walls

Courts

Softening roof lines

Shade

Background and enframement

Integration

Stability

Note: Numbers following plant names represent height plants will grow, along with the best exposure to place plants. Exposure listed first is the best exposure for the optimum health and appearance of the plant.

Alnus glutinosa [European Alder] 30' Sun or Shade. Picturesque in habit, persistent catkins. Catkins and cone-like fruit add interest.

Acer rubrum [Red Maple] 50' Sun or Shade. Recognized for excellent fall foliage color. Color is orange red.

Acer saccharum [Sugar Maple] 50' Sun. Excellent fall foliage color and uniform growth. Slow growing.

Cercidiphyllum japonicum [Katsura Tree] 35' Sun. Small heart shaped leaves with purple and gold fall foliage color.

Fagus sylvatica [European Beech] 50' Sun or Shade. Stately tree with smooth gray bark. Rich green foliage turning golden color in fall. Long pointed winter buds add interest.

Ginkgo biloba [Ginkgo] 50' Sun or Light Shade. A tree for strength in the garden. Various habits of growth. Interesting leaves. Free of plant pests.

Liquidambar styraciflua [Sweet Gum] 50' Sun. Star shaped leaves. Good fall foliage color. Interesting nut like fruit.

Phellodendron amurense [Amur Cork Tree] 30' Sun. Broad headed tree with compound leaves. Blue black berries.

Red Maple

Quercus palustris [Pin Oak] 50' Sun or Shade. A stately tree of pyramid habit. Excellent fall foliage color.

DECIDUOUS SHRUBS

FOR   *Background*

   Separating areas

   Hedges

   Integration

Aronia arbutifolia [Red Chokeberry] 5' Sun or Shade. Erect shrub with pinkish tinged white flowers excellent fall foliage color. Persistent red berries.

Aesculus parviflora [Bottlebrush Buckeye] 6' Shade. Horizontal branching habit. Grows wider than tall. Mound like appearance. White flowers in July.

Amelanchier stolonifera [Running Serviceberry] 4' Shade or Sun. Low growing shrub, naturalistic in appearance. Plum colored berries. Good fall foliage color.

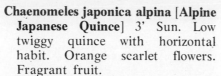

Dwarf Korean Lilac

Winged Euonymus

Korean Spice Bush

Chaenomeles japonica alpina [Alpine Japanese Quince] 3' Sun. Low twiggy quince with horizontal habit. Orange scarlet flowers. Fragrant fruit.

Cotoneaster apiculata [Cranberry Cotoneaster] 3' Sun. Horizontal branching mound like appearance. Small waxy leaves with persistent red berries.

Cotoneaster adpressa praecox [Early Cotoneaster] 3' Sun. A low grower with fine leaves and brilliant red berries.

Cotoneaster divaricata [Spreading Cotoneaster] 5' Sun. Graceful in habit. Small leaves and red berries. Excellent fall foliage color.

Cornus officinalis [Japanese Cornelian Cherry Dogwood] 15' Shade or Sun. Interesting branching structure. Yellow flowers in March. Red fruit in fall. Exfoliating bark and roundish buds add interest.

Euonymus yedoensis [Yeddo Euonymus] 10' Sun. Semi arborescent branching, bold foliage

Forsythia

Flowering Quince

with decorative rose colored fruit. Fall foliage color is red.

Euonymus europeus [European Euonymus] 15' Sun. Leathery dark green foliage, pink capsules in autumn that open and expose attractive orange seeds.

Euonymus alatus [Winged Euonymus] 12' Sun. Horizontal branching, corky bark with rose pink fall foliage color.

Euonymus alatus compactus [Dwarf Burning Bush] 5' Sun. Dwarf form of Euonymus. Bright red fall foliage color. Upright habit. Narrower at base of plant.

Forsythia virdissima bronxensis [Dwarf Forsythia] 15' Sun. Low growing vertical branched forsythia. Dense growth. Mound like habit. Attractive saw toothed leaves. Yellow leaves.

Hamamelis mollis brevipetala [Chinese Witchhazel] 10' Shade or Sun. Gray green leaves. Blooms from March to early April. Bright yellow flowers.

Ilex verticillata [Winterberry] 5' Sun or Shade. A deciduous holly noted for its profuse red berries.

Kerria japonica [Japanese Kerry Bush] 4' Shade or Sun. Slender stems of brightest green for winter interest. Flowers are yellow in May.

Prunus tomentosa [Nanking Cherry] 8' Sun or Shade. Flowers are pink in bud opening to white. Flowers produce a transparent cherry in late spring.

Rhus aromatica [Fragrant Sumac] 5' Sun or Shade. Yellow flowering shrub that blooms in May. Aromatic foliage. Excellent fall foliage color. Small fuzzy berry. Naturalistic in appearance.

Rhamnus frangula columnaris [Columnar Buckthorn] 12' Sun or Shade. A narrow growing shrub to a width of four feet. Vertical branching. Excellent for areas where space is limited. Good fall foliage color and abundant berries.

Rhus typhina laciniata [Cut Leaf Sumac] 10' Sun or Shade. Irregular habit of growth. Excellent fine textured foliage that has a superb fall color.

Viburnum carlesi [Korean Spice Viburnum] 6' Sun. The best shrub for fragrant flowers. Berries are reddish purple. Fall foliage color is attractive.

Viburnum plicatum tomentosum [Double file Viburnum] 6'-8' Sun or Shade. Horizontal branching with attractive foliage and creamy white flower clusters. Flowers are arranged in flat planes at the upper surfaces and they are most charming.

NEEDLED EVERGREENS

FOR *Accents*

Year around effect

Privacy

Ground cover

Background

Integration

Abies lasiocarpa arizonica [Blue Cork Bark Fir] 30' Sun. A blue needled form of the Arizona fir. Spongy creamy white bark is interesting.

Cedrus atlantica [Atlas Cedar] 30' Sun. Attractive blue gray needles. Habit of growth is somewhat irregular and interesting.

Cryptomeria japonica [Japanese Cypress] 35' Sun. Tall arrow type habit with dark green needles.

Juniperus horizontalis [Blue Rug] 6"

Pinus cembra [Swiss Stone Pine] 30' Sun. A slow growing pine with a narrow habit and exquisite charm.

Pinus strobus [White Pine] 35' Sun or Shade. A stately pine with soft, fine textured needles.

Pinus densiflora umbraculifera [Japanese Umbrella Pine] 20' Sun. A many stemmed pine with brownish red exfoliating bark. Flat topped appearance creates a magnificent look.

Pinus parviflora [Japanese White Pine] 35' Sun. Wide spreading with a horizontal branching habit. Tufted clusters of dark green needles. Attractive cones.

Pinus thunbergi [Japanese Black Pine] 35' Sun. Variable picturesque shapes. Blackish gray deeply fissured bark that is interesting. Enjoys a light soil.

Pinus flexilis [Limber Pine] 20' Sun. Dark green needles, flexible branches, and a branching habit that is irregular.

Pinus nigra [Austrian Pine] 30' Sun. Stiff dark green needles. Habit is upright and has a rugged appearance.

Pinus sylvestris [Scotch Pine] 30' Sun. Fast growing pine with short needles, wind swept appearance in later years, and attractive orange bark.

Pseudotsuga taxifolia [Douglas Fir] 35' Sun or Shade. Soft needled evergreen with dark green to silvery blue foliage. Excellent conifer.

Taxus cuspidata densiformis [Newport Yew] 30" Shade or Sun. Semi-dwarf yew with thick light green needles. Compact habit.

Taxus cuspidata nana [Dwarf Yew] 2' Shade or Sun. Slow growing and low growing evergreen with thick dark green needles. Excellent appearance.

Mugho Pine

Bar Harbor Juniper

Sun. Mat like growth. Use as espalier, ground cover or cascading over a wall. Extremely attractive blue foliage.

Juniperus chinensis [San Jose] 12" Sun. Attractive blue green creeping juniper for ground covering and in conjunction with rock outcroppings.

Juniperus chinensis [Sargent] 15" Sun. Dark green creeping juniper with ground hugging ability.

Juniperus procumbens nana [Dwarf Japanese Juniper] 15" Sun. Horizontal growth with bluish green foliage. Dense growth and extremely attractive.

Pinus mugho mughus [Dwarf Mugho Pine] 2' Sun. Mound like growth when pruned annually.

Taxus media Hicks [Hicks Yew] 5'
Shade or Sun. Columnar growth
for low hedges and division of areas
in the landscape.

Tsuga canadensis [Canadian Hemlock] 35' Shade or Sun.
Picturesque fine needled evergreen
with graceful drooping branches
and delightful small cones.

Tsuga canadensis prostrata [Creeping Eastern Hemlock] 2'
Shade or Sun. Flat growing
evergreen for ground cover and
underplanting small deciduous
trees.

Thuja occidentalis Holmstrupp [Holmstrupp Arborvitae] 4' Sun.
Low dwarf evergreen for a
diminutive effect. Slow growing.

Thuja occidentalis Techny [Mission Arborvitae] 12' Sun or Shade. A
tall growing arborvitae for
screening and living walls.

Canadian Hemlock   [Pendulant Form]

Techny Arborvitae

Scotch Pine.

BROADLEAF EVERGREENS

FOR   *Shady areas*

Contrast

Hedges

Integration

Ground cover

Buxus microphylla koreana [Korean Little Leaf Boxwood] 2' Shade or Semi-shade. Dense broadleaf evergreen with small leaves. Excellent for diminutive dividers.

Buxus sempervirens [English Boxwood] 10' Shade or Semi-shade. Taller growing boxwood for larger areas and tall screens.

Euonymus fortunei coloratus [Purple Leaf Wintercreeper] 2' Shade or Sun. Similar to bigleaf wintercreeper but without berries. Foliage turns a plum color during late fall and winter.

Euonymus fortunei kewensis [Kew Wintercreeper] 3" Shade or Semi-shade. Mat-like growth with tiny leaves.

Euonymus fortunei vegetus [Bigleaf Wintercreeper] 2' Shade or Semi-shade. Waxy green leaves, orange berries and a handsome appearance. Use as climbing vine or ground cover.

Hedera helix baltica [Baltic Ivy] 6" Shade. Evergreen ground cover or vine with attractive dark green leaves. This evergreen vine has the ability to climb and adhere to walls or trees.

Ilex crenata convexa [Japanese Convex-leaf Holly] 6' Shade or Semi-shade. Waxy leaves, black berries, and attractive the year around.

Oregon Grape Holly

Leucothoe cataesbaei [Drooping Leucothoe] 4' Shade. A two-toned foliaged shrub with maroon-green leaves and drooping creamy flowers.

Mahonia aquifolium [Oregon Grape Holly] 5' Shade. A two-toned leafy evergreen, maroon and green with yellow flowers and attractive blue berries.

Pachysandra terminalis [Japanese Spurge] 8" Shade or Sun. Evergreen ground cover adapting to shade as well as sunny locations. Use under small trees and difficult areas.

Japanese Andromeda

Rhododendron

Pachistima canbyi [Pachistima] 12" Sun or Light Shade. Low growing waxy-leaved ground cover for sunny well-drained situations. Small leaves.

Pieris japonica [Japanese Pieris] 8' Shade or Semi-shade. Shrubby evergreen with attractive waxy leaves, and white flowers that are a cascading delight to see in April.

Rhododendron [Numerous varieties] 3'-12' Shade or Semi-shade. Leafy evergreens with attractive foliage and spectacular flowers.

Vinca minor [Periwinkle] 6" Shade. Shiny foliage with blue flowers in spring. Use under trees and in mass where shade is available.

Azalea Mollis

Boxwood

HERBACEOUS PERENNIALS

FOR *Ground cover*

Rock associations

Integration

Arenaria balearica [Sandwort] 3″ Semi-shade. Moss—like ground cover for use with rocks in semi-shaded areas.

Asarum canadense [Wild Ginger] 6″ Shade. A cool spot in the garden is the place for Wild Ginger. Large roundish bright green leaves make this plant worthwhile.

Adiantum pedatum [Maidenhair Fern] 18″ Shade. A shade loving fern with lovely textured foliage.

Houstonia caerulea [Bluets] 3″ Shade. Tufted perennial for the shade. Blue or white flowers. Mat-like appearance.

Iberis sempervirens [Candytuft] 10″ Sun. Mound-like growth with white flowers in spring. Evergreen-like foliage that is extremely attractive.

Sedum [Stone crop varieties] 3″-20″ Sun. Mostly ground-hugging, flowering and attractive foliage.

Thymus serphyllum [Mother of Thyme] 3″ Sun. An herb with a delightful scent and mat-like growth. Use near walks and rocks.

Hosta decorata marginata [Funkia or Plantain Lily] 18″ Shade or Sun. Narrow-leaved plant with white along the margins.

Artemesia schmidtiana [Silver Mound] 12″ Sun. Smoky appearing foliage of a silvery-gray color.

Iris laevigata [Japanese Iris] 10″ Sun or Shade. Slender leaves and large flowers. Enjoys the water's edge.

Artemisia

Sedum

Candy Tuft

DECIDUOUS VINES

FOR *Ground cover*

Fences

Walls

Trees

Integration

Celastrus scandens [American Bittersweet] 30′ Sun or Shade. Twining vine of vigorous habit and yellow-coated, orange-red fruit in late summer. Foliage is golden in fall.

Hydrangea petiolaris [Climbing Hydrangea] 30′ Shade. Waxy leaves and white flowers in mid-June.

Parthenocissus quinquefolia [Woodbine] 40′ Sun. Blue-fruited vine with brilliant fall foliage color.

Boston Ivy

Bittersweet

GRASS OR GRASS LIKE PLANTS

FOR *Accents*

Effect

Contrast

Elymus glaucus [Blue Lime Grass] 2' Sun. Blue foliage with vigorous spreading habit. Use in restricted areas with rocks, lanterns, wood structures, and wood benches.

Festuca ovina glauca [Blue Mist fescue] 6" Sun. A low growing fine bladed grass with a tuft-like appearance. Blue foliage.

Phalaris arundinacea picta [Ribbon Grass] 2' Sun. Green and yellow striped blades. Vigorous growth.

Yucca filamentosa [Adam's Needle] 30" Sun. Year around interest. A bold grass with sword like blades. Appearance is dramatic. Tall spiked white flowers in late spring.

Cyperus papyrus [Paper Plant] 5' Sun or Light Shade. Paper plant grows in or out of water. Best appearance when used in ponds. Not hardy North. Treat as a house plant during cold months.

Yucca

DECIDUOUS SMALL TREES
(Preferably multiple stem)

FOR *Accent*

Entrances

Spacious walls

Courts

Soften roof lines

Dimension

Integration

Acer tataricum [Tatarian Maple] 20' Sun or Shade. This small tree has excellent fall color. Use near and with shrubs and ground cover.

Acer ginnala [Amur Maple] 20' Sun or Shade. A brown-barked maple with attractively lobed leaves that turn orange-red in fall.

Acer palmatum [Japanese Maple] 20' Shade or Sun. Green and red-leafed forms are part of this species. There is also a cut-leafed form. Trees are smooth-barked

Sargent Crabapple

and have superior branching structures.

Amelanchier canadensis [Service-berry] 20' Ascending branching habit. Gray smooth bark and white flowers in early spring, purplish-red berries follow. Good fall foliage color.

Betula nigra [River Birch] 35' Shade or Sun. Shaggy orange tan bark. Tolerates moist situations.

Carpinus caroliniana [American Hornbeam] 25' Shade. Irregular growing habit. Interesting bark and burnt-orange fall foliage color.

Cercis canadensis [Eastern Redbud] 25' Shade or Sun. Dark bark, lavender colored flowers before the leaves in spring.

Chionanthus virginicus [White Fringe Tree] 25' Sun. Large waxy looking leaves, large white fragrant flowers. Fruit is dark blue.

Cornus alternifolia [Pagoda Dogwood] 20' Shade or Sun. A tiered branching habit with smooth reddish bark, white flowers in mid-spring, and blue berries add to the charm of this small tree.

Cornus florida [Flowering Dogwood] 25' Shade or Sun. A picturesque tree with large white branch-like flowers in early spring. Fruit is red and foliage color is spectacular in fall.

Cornus kousa [Kousa Dogwood] 30' Shade or Sun. Pink fruiting dogwood with strong interesting branch and trunk structure.

Crataegus crus-galli [Cockspur Hawthorn] 20' Sun. Horizontally branched red-berried hawthorn with waxy leaves and excellent fall foliage color. Wine-colored fruit.

Pink Dogwood

Crataegus phaenopyrum [Washington Hawthorn] 20' Sun. Narrow-growing hawthorn. Excellent fall foliage color. Persistent orange-red berries.

Cladrastis lutea [Yellowwood] 25' Sun. Silvery-colored smooth bark and white pendulous flowers in June.

Halesia caroliniana [Carolina Silverbell] 25' Sun. White bell-shaped flowers. Striped bark. Foliage is golden in fall.

Hamamelis virginiana [Common Witchhazel] 15' Shade or Sun. Yellow flowers in October and November. Fall foliage color is golden to bronze.

Larix leptolepis [Japanese Larch] 35' Sun or Shade. Decorative checkered bark. Short soft needles that turn a soft brown in fall.

Magnolia stellata [Star Magnolia] 10' Sun or Shade. Fragrant star-shaped flowers in early spring.

Metasequoia glyptostroboides [Dawn Redwood] 35' Sun. Fast growing deciduous conifer with soft green fine-textured foliage that turns copper color in the fall.

Malus Red Jade [Red Jade Weeping Crabapple] 12' Sun. Flowers are pink in bud opening to white in spring. Fruit is pea-size and red. Outstanding weeping tree for the garden.

Malus floribunda [Japanese Flowering Crabapple] 25' Sun or Shade. Flowers pink in bud opening to white. Fruit is pea-size and yellow. Picturesque habit.

Malus hupehensis [Tea Crab] 20' Sun or Shade. Ascending narrow habit, white or pink flowers that are fragrant. Fruit is yellow.

Malus sargenti [Sargent Crabapple] 8' Sun. A superior small tree, wider than tall. Flowers are white and fruit is wine-colored.

Malus zumi calocarpa [Japanese Zumi Crabapple] 25' Sun or Light Shade. Branching structure is interesting, flowers are pink in bud and open to white. Berries are red or yellow and persistent.

Oxydendron arboreum [Sourwood] 35' Sun. Narrow and irregularly-branched tree with waxy foliage, orange-red fall foliage and small white flowers in July or August.

Ostrya virginiana [Ironwood] 30' Shade or Sun. Sturdy tree with exfoliating bark and interesting nut-like catkins.

Prunus sargenti [Sargent Cherry] 30' Sun or Shade. A smooth reddish-barked tree with bronze-colored leaves as they unfold in the spring, followed by large pink flowers.

Prunus subhirtella pendula [Weeping Higan Cherry] 12' Sun. Pink flowers in spring. Fine textured weeping branches.

Photina villosa [Oriental Photina] 20' Sun or Light Shade. Excellent structural tree, bright red fruit, and bronze-red fall foliage.

Syringa amurensis japonica [Japanese Tree Lilac] 18' Sun or Light Shade. Shiny cherry like bark, feathery panicles of creamy white flowers in late June.

Above: Zumi Calocarpa Crabapple
Below: Magnolia Stellata [blossoms]

Left: Redbud

INDEX